# Account Security Basics

First Printing, 2016

Idea Seed Labs, Inc
4635 S Norfolk Way
Aurora, CO 80015

www.AuthorBillPrice.com

the law.

**Pursuant to the Federal Trade Commission Guidelines:**

**MATERIAL CONNECTION DISCLOSURE:**

The publisher of this book may be or does have an affiliate relationship and/or another material connection to the providers of goods and services mentioned in this book and may be compensated when you purchase from any of the links contained herein.

You should always perform due diligence before buying goods or services from anyone via the Internet or "off-line".

# Table of Contents

## Preface (READ FIRST!)

While this guide may often focus on e-mail accounts, all of the information presented within this entire course can be applied across the board (and web) to any account or website that supports ANY of the security features or topics mentioned in the following pages.

If you really think about it, the basis of account creation (in most cases), links back to your e-mail account in some way. It's like your social security number in a way, but perhaps not AS extreme. It's something you often identify with and use to verify yourself or communicate around the world.

So, again, while a lot of the focus in this course is on the e-mail account aspect of account security, this knowledge is completely universal and not in any way exclusive to JUST e-mail service providers or accounts.

It is just insinuated that the root of everything should be the security of your e-mail, so the main goal is to keep that account as secure and safe guarded as possible. And of course, amongst that, also being strict about the security of any and all other accounts you create on the web.

Without further a due, let's get right into it...

Email itself is much older than even ARPANet or the Internet. It was never actually invented; it simply evolved from very simple beginnings.

Early email was just a small advance on what we know these days as a file directory - it just put a message in another user's directory in a spot where they could see it when they logged in. Simple as that. Just like leaving a note on someone's desk.

Probably the first email system of this type was MAILBOX, used at Massachusetts Institute of Technology from 1965. Another early program to send messages on the same computer was called SNDMSG.

Some of the mainframe computers of this era might have had up to one hundred users -often they used what are called "dumb terminals" to access the mainframe from their work desks. Dumb terminals just connected to the mainframe - they had no storage or memory of their own, they did all their work on the remote mainframe computer.

Before internet-working began, therefore, email could only be used to send messages to various users of the same computer. Once computers began to talk to each other over networks, however, the problem became a little more complex - We needed to be able to put a message in an envelope and address it. To do this, we needed a means to indicate to whom letters should go that the electronic posties understood - just like the postal system, we needed a way to indicate an address.

This is why Ray Tomlinson is credited with inventing email in 1972. Like many of the Internet inventors, Tomlinson worked for Bolt Beranek and Newman as an ARPANET contractor. He picked the @ symbol from the computer keyboard to denote sending messages from one computer to another.

So then, for anyone using Internet standards, it was simply a matter of nominating name-of-the-user@name-of-the-computer. Internet pioneer Jon Postel, was one of the first users of the new system, and is credited with describing it as a "nice hack". It certainly was, and it has lasted to this day.

Despite what the world wide web offers, email remains the most important application of the Internet and the most widely used facility it has.

It's really no surprise that now more than 3 BILLION people internationally use email for some purpose or another.

G-mail alone has quoted over 300 million users just a few years ago.

Even crazier is that MILLIONS of email users send

HUNDREDS of BILLIONS of messages every single day.

## Account Security Introduction

With all of this email activity and people using email, have you ever considered the security of your email account?

Imagine this:

You use your smart-phone to receive emails regularly. You are out to dinner and all of a sudden you receive a notification that there's been a suspicious log-in on your email account.

Your stomach is in knots by the time you finish reading the message. You gulp down your meal and rush to a computer. It's already too late. Your account has been jeopardized.

Now you have to spend hours (and days) trying to re-claim and secure your personal information like your bank and credit card accounts, PayPal or other payment processing accounts, social media accounts, business accounts (and messages) and so much more.

Most people think that it couldn't happen to them, but it's actually far more common than you would believe...

Think about everywhere that your email account may be used to sign up for accounts, or even plastered publicly due to poor privacy settings in various networks (not your fault though).

Consider what might happen if someone were to gain access to a pool of usernames and passwords that signed up for something like say, a forum. They might then run through the email accounts connected to the usernames, and try the specified password for each.

This could spell catastrophe for you, not to mention all of the other people as well.

The thing is, you can easily take a few seemingly simple precautions to secure your account immensely. Putting into practice just a few techniques and setting up a few things on the back end, and you can lower the chances of a successful attack from a hacker an infinite amount.

Furthermore, if you take the time to secure your account (and associated accounts - as you'll see), then in the event that your account is compromised, you will easily have the tools and skills to swiftly reclaim your account and your privacy as well.

Passwords...

The password itself doesn't need an explanation, as you already know what it is.

The real question is: do you have a secure enough password?

Generally speaking, if your password contains any ordinary word, especially by itself - it probably isn't AS secure as it could be.

That's not to say that your password isn't secure right now, it very well may be.

But if it's simply a word like "animal" or even "password" (you'd be surprised!) then you're really at huge risk.

Even adding a number to your password, like "animal22" or "password123" isn't safe anymore. Password crackers (software that cycles through passwords at a fast pace) can run through different combinations with ease in just a short period of time.  If somebody truly wanted to get into your account, they could even quickly run through weird variations like "ani2mal2" or "1pass2word3" with a little bit of ambition (towards breaking into your account).

Enough talk about weak passwords, let's cover how you can improve your current password or even generate a new password.

In most cases, passwords are case sensitive.  You can use this to your advantage in a lot of ways.

Better yet, nowadays a lot of services will allow you to insert symbols into your password now too.

(The Following Is Just An Example)

This means that you can turn a password like "fastcar" into "!(faSt22CAR)!" and it will work flawlessly. Yes, that's an annoying password to type in, and maybe even to remember. But think of how much effort it may take to crack a password like that.

As it is, that kind of methodology could be enough to secure your password, BUT if you want to really step it up a notch and keep things essentially UNCRACKABLE - then you want to generate a completely random password.

If you want to go the old fashion way, you can just come up with something random such as the following examples:

1. 84q7d*2e55YD
2. 709i!F7B7D2D
3. vb91Xd6*7R64

Those are really complex and may be difficult to

remember. But just keep in mind this is your security you're talking about and that goes a long way.

You don't have to go that complex either. A few capital and lower case letters, a few numbers, and a symbol or two. That's all it takes to make it secure.

If you want to have it all done for you, there are plenty of services out there that will help generate a password for you (along these lines):

- https://lastpass.com/generatepassword.php + [ Quick and easy, click a button and you get an incredibly random and safe to use password. ]
- http://passwordsgenerator.net/ + [ Complex and very customizable. Use this if you want to step up every bit of your password and even passphrase security with minimal effort. ]
- https://www.random.org/passwords/ + [ Enter some information and click a button, and you have your randomized password generated. ]

Lastly, sometimes the account registration page found

within the sign up process (for a service) will have a bar that will tell you the security of your password, graded on a poor, medium, secure scale.

There are even services that require you to have X amount of capital letters, numbers, and symbols in your password to even proceed with the registration.

So that just enforces the ideal that having a very secure password for not just your email account, but any account, is the way forward now and in the future.

**IMPORTANT:** Never use a universal password for all of your accounts, meaning using the same password for every account or multiple "meant to be secure" accounts. Regardless of if it's e-mail or other accounts. Especially for forums and other registrations.

I will discuss more in depth about this topic later on.

## Account Security Questions...

The account security question (often referred to by other names) is simply a 2-step authentication method and account recovery method used by most e-mail service providers and other network providers as well.

There are 2 main instances in which your account security question will be displayed and require an answer...

1. You will often be required to answer this question upon logging into your e-mail account from an unknown (or new) Internet connection / location.

2. This question will also be displayed and require an answer in the event that you want to reset the password for your e-mail account.

Because of this, malicious individuals can use this method to gain access to your account by resetting the password if they can easily decipher the answer to your security question.

When it comes to actually choosing a question and answer, you have to put some thought into it.

The reality is that any honest answer that you choose, may be posing a security threat to your account.

Unfortunately, this is due in part to the fact that there is just a lot of personal information out there about us, maybe some more than others.

Whether it's Facebook, Twitter, Google+, LinkedIn, or another network - or maybe even someone that knows personal information about you in your life (vindictive relationships that end, and so on).

All of these factors should ultimately play into the question and answer you choose.

With that said, it's really a lot easier for YOU to come up with an exclusive and safe account security answer than it may sound. Most times, you'll be forced to choose from a standard set (list) of questions, and then most people would just enter the honest answer.

That's where the danger exists. The Internet and those with malicious intent have many ways of digging up information about you.

There's a few ways that you can attack the "default question" situation.

1. Get creative with it. Instead of answering what your "home town" really is; enter a city that you've always loved. Make sure you remember that though!

2. Use a random password / pass phrase for this

answer instead of just answering the question normally. It's important that you can remember this answer. The next part discusses more in depth about how you can do this.

In other cases, you may be able to choose your question and the answer. This is where you can send any potential "hackers" for a confusing loop. Instead of using a question; use a phrase that reminds you of something else. Then choose the "something else" as the answer.

As a (lame) example to the custom question, you may have a favorite food. That food may have some ingredient that stands out the most, that you really enjoy.

Let's say you love BLTs (bacon, lettuce and tomato sandwiches). Going from that, think of something broad that could mean anything, like BACON.

You can have "Bacon?" as the question, and then have

"BLT" as the answer. Something similar to that.

You could even add your favorite number(s) to the end of that to make it even more confusing and exclusive. So in that case, the question could be "Bacon Numbers?" and the answer would be "BLT44" or whatever your favorite number may be.

Obviously the above is just an example, but it should spark some creative ideas that allow you to really secure your email account from any potential break-in attempts via guessing the account security question's answer.

There may also be rare instances where you can bypass the creation of the security question. While this may seem convenient, it can lead to disaster later on down the road - especially if you end up forgetting your password.

It's STRONGLY advised that you take the extra time to choose a security question and an answer at the creation of your account so as to not end up forgetting later on in the future.

Emergency / Recovery / Secondary Accounts...

It doesn't matter what they're referred to, they all direct to the same thing: a backup email account.

When registering a new account, whether it's for an email account or a random website, often times you will be asked to provide a backup / emergency email account.

This could be used for a number of instances...

- Account / Password Recovery
- Password Reset Process
- Accessing from another location (multi-step authentication)
- (Sometimes) Changing important information about your account (password, security question, etc)

Regardless of the scenario in which you NEED to use this account, there's a few things you need to come in mind when creating or choosing an emergency / backup account.

First off, what is the relationship of the secondary account to your first account? Does it share any of the same credentials such as password or security question answer? Do they link to each other (for back up accounts, also a terrible idea)?

Ideally, you want this secondary account to remain a complete secret. Don't use it to sign up for things and don't link it to a ton of accounts. Above all, don't use the same credentials for the account. It should have no relation to your main account (the account for which it's serving as an emergency, backup).

This is an account that you want to ALWAYS remember

the log-in details for, and keep heavily safe guarded.

In the event that a disaster strikes, you want to be capable of quickly accessing this back-up account and/or trying to use this account to reset the compromised account details (password, security question, etc).

By ensuring that these 2 accounts have no relation, other than one being used as the recovery to the other, you greatly decrease the risk of having your main email account compromised permanently. As you will be able to reset and gain access to the account but requesting reset details to your backup account.

## Adding Your Mobile Number...

If your email provider, or even any website with pertinent information on it, allows you the opportunity to connect your mobile phone number as an extra level of security for your account - it is HIGHLY recommended that you take advantage of this option.

While you may be wary about actually sharing THAT personal of information with a service, provider, or website, there's a main reason why you don't usually have to be. When a company offers this feature in terms of account security and a layer of protection, they generally have EXTREMELY SAFE methods for storing and protecting your mobile phone number.

Generally the process plays out as such...

1. Enter your number & choose "Call" with a code or "Text" with a code.
2. Click the "Send" or "Call" button.
3. Enter the code provided to you.
4. Click confirm, and wait.

Your account should be confirmed and connected to your mobile phone number after that (general) process.

This is important because many times you may be able to enable mobile authentication from foreign locations (as mentioned before and will be many times). This means that you can be alerted via mobile any time there's something going on with your account that may be out of the ordinary.

Building on top of that, you can often use your mobile number as a means to reset or gain access to said (connected) account in the event that you happen to lose access, your account is stolen or compromised, or you simply forget your password.

Any time you have the opportunity to add or connect a mobile phone to a pertinent account, you should definitely consider doing such.

Aside from regularly logging into your email account, and 2-step authentication, there's a couple other ways to check up on activity (suspicious or not) within your email account.

Starting off, you should of course have the mobile notifications enabled for ANY email account that you use or even own. You should already have a mobile number attached to your account for security purposes, as mentioned earlier

This is just taking it a step further to let you know any time anything may happen on your account. Often times this is located in the settings page of any email service provider that actually supports it.

Another thing to keep in mind...

Some email services (and even other websites like Facebook) allow you to monitor the recent log in activity on your account. This will display the IP address and location of the last few connection / log-ins to your email account

.

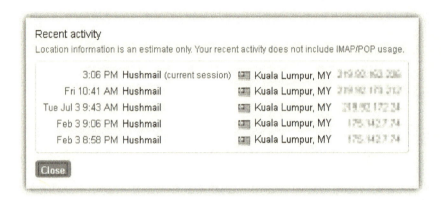

Lastly, you should always check your "Sent" messages folder at least once a week. This is to ensure that there's no suspicious messages being sent out, which would insinuate that someone may have access to your account and be using it carefully.

You've probably seen them before. You've received a payment from an ancestor you never knew of, and it's being held in some bank in another country. You just have to click this link, or confirm these details, or send a small payment.

It doesn't really matter what kind of message you've received or that you've heard of - they're all mostly considering phishing, and they're ALL scams of some sort. Sometimes they may just be asking you for personal information; which in MOST cases, MOST people would immediately close the email, or not even open the email to begin with.

Other times there may be a link in the body of the email. Clicking this link may direct you to a page where you fill out information, or even worse - a page that has a malicious script executed in the background upon page load. This is how hackers use a "backdoor" to gain entrance to your computer or accounts.

I won't go into detail regarding back doors but if you want to learn more, read this link: http://computersecurity.wikia.com/wiki/Backdoor.

There's all kinds of ways for scammers to attack your email inbox, whether it's just a request for personal information or a "small" fee, or sending you a malicious link. It's important that you learn to avoid all of these scenarios by keeping an eye out and getting in the habit of recognizing spam messages.

While you may think that this topic is trivial because most people would already know this information, you would be flabbergasted at the amount of new email users that ends of falling for these scams and spam.

Ordinarily when you receive a link, you can hover your cursor over the link and a tool-tip will display with the target URL. This allows you to be certain that the link you're clicking is really sending you to that location.

When it comes to e-mail, senders are able to embed a link that points to another target URL. They can even use link cloaking / forwarding services to disguise their link.

Because of this, you don't always know where you could be sent when you click on a link. That can be potentially very dangerous.

Fortunately, this a way to "vet" links that you receive to determine if they're malicious or legitimate.

It's not a difficult task to quickly check a link and see if it's malicious. For starters, you already should know that hovering over a link will display a tooltip with it's true location.

Beyond that, the nature of the email should really tell you a lot about the intent of the link found within the message. If the email seems suspicious, then the link is most likely suspicious as well.

Additionally, you shouldn't even click the link just out of curiosity. Believe it or not, some individuals have done that and it can yield disastrous results. So, don't take risks!

Often times, the email address that sends you a malicious link or message will have a strange address as it is. They frequently have a strange subject line, and the formatting of the message is suspect as well.

There's a number of free services that can take it a step further and really scan a URL to check if it's safe or not.

1. http://scanurl.net/ - [ This is an excellent and fast resource to quickly scan links. ]
2. https://safeweb.norton.com/ - [ Another free link / website scanner, but this time it's from Norton. ]

You don't really have to use these services for every single link that you encounter. However, you should save them for times when you are just completely not sure.

Perhaps when a friend sends you a link and you believe their account may have been compromised, and so on.

None of this is very complicated or difficult, and you can easily get in the habit of recognizing bad links and messages. Eventually you won't even have to open the emails to know if they're spam, just by the subject line.

One of the many features offered to all users of the Avast Free Antivirus software is a fully functional e-mail shield. When enabled, the program will scan all incoming messages and outgoing messages for viruses and other types of malware that may be hiding as attachments.

You can both enable and configure this feature at any time using tools already available to you in the main Avast Free Antivirus program window. No additional software downloads are required to get this feature off the ground.

Many individuals have this enabled to add another additional layer of security to their accounts.

## How To Tell If An Email Is Legitimate

There's a few ways to recognize if an email might be suspicious. Here's just a brief list that can help you out.

— Any email requesting that you take action on an

account or provide personal information via e-mail, may be suspicious and should most times not be trusted

- Never click directly on links in an e-mail, hover over them first to check
- If an e-mail asks you to submit confidential information via another form or an outbound page, this is generally not safe and is a phishing attempt
- Any time you have a suspicion, you should contact the support team or support desk / contact for the company in question
- If the e-mail is caught in a spam or trash filter and it looks like it may be coming from a suspicious address (reply-to), then it should be avoided

After the initial setup phase of an email account, you generally won't have to worry about much spam.

As the time goes on though, you will start to encounter more and more spam messages. It's just the cycle of using email.

Sometimes a website that you signed up for will end up selling the email list for their site (to make some money - and yes, that's technically not legal to do). Other times, you may have posted your e-mail address somewhere and it was "scraped" from an automated bot (software).

Regardless of how it happens, you may be getting unwanted messages. The issue is that it's not always so simple to get rid of those messages once and for all. Because if you click an "unsubscribe" link (if there even is one) in the email, you could end up being directed somewhere else that tells the sender that it's an active email. You could get added to dozens more email lists at minimum, and that means MORE SPAM and unwanted messages in your inbox.

The good thing is that a lot of email service providers will allow you to create what are called "filters" to automatically sort messages that you may not want to see.

Finding the filters options in your e-mail provider is different for every one of them, but generally can be found in the settings or preferences.

In our case, we will use GMail (Google Mail) to show you how to create a filter.

1. To create a filter, all you need to do is type any keyword, email address, or anything you want to search for, in the search box at the top of your GMail window.

2. Before clicking "Search", simply click the down arrow on the right side of the input box.

3. It will roll down another small options window, and at the bottom right side, you should see "Create filter with this search >>" - Simply click that link.

4. From there, you simply select the options (see image below) that you want to apply to these filters. In the case of unwanted messages and spam, you can choose to "Delete it" as soon as it hits your inbox.

dating

« back to search options                                                    ×

When a message arrives that matches this search:

☐ Skip the Inbox (Archive it)
☐ Mark as read
☐ Star it
☐ Apply the label:  Choose label... ⬍
☐ Forward it to:  Choose an address... ⬍      add forwarding address
☐ Delete it
☐ Never send it to Spam
☐ Always mark it as important
☐ Never mark it as important
☐ Categorize as:  Choose category... ⬍

[Create filter]   ☐ Also apply filter to matching messages.

Learn more

That's really all there is to it when it comes to creating
filters. The process is similar to every email service
provider, but you may just have to do a quick search or
help query for your provider to figure out how to create a
filter.

Keep in mind that they may be referred to as something
different depending on who provides your email service to
you.

** **NOTE:** Another cool suggestion that is highly recommended if you want to keep your inbox organized and tidy is to make use of "folders" or "labels" (depends on your provider). These are simply sections where you can archive e-mail messages that you receive.

You can also create filters that automatically mark e-mails from certain people or with specified keywords and add label them accordingly. This allows you to make the overall email usage process a lot more seamless and less stressful. In turn, you can focus more on potential out of the ordinary messages and activity.

---

## Checking Spam And Trash folders Regularly (For Messages Accidentally Caught In Spam Filters)

A lot of email service providers have built-in spam filters set up to automatically make your experience more seamlessly and less confusing. These filters might catch phrases that almost ALWAYS spam related or even filter messages based on email address (sender).

Most times, this is an asset to your email experience. However, occasionally it will slip up and catch an email message that you actually wanted to receive in your inbox. Things like confirmation emails from forums and other websites often have this happen.

Other times, it could even be from somebody who you know that was trying to get in contact with you but has never emailed you before. Or they may have unintentionally used a "spam" word and because of that, the email provider instantly marked their messages as spam to save you the hassle.

So... how do you get around this?

There's a few methods, one of which I will cover more in detail later on in this course.

For now, the easiest way to go about finding these messages is to regularly (once a week or more) check both your spam and trash folders for your e-mail account.

A quick skim through the sender addresses and the subject lines should usually tell you if it's something important that slipped through the cracks.

In the event that you find an email that wasn't supposed to end up in the trash or spam, there's a simple remedy.

First, you can just create a filter with that sender's email address and tell it to NEVER mark as spam or send to the trash.

You can also add that person to your "Address Book" which most email service providers will have built-in to your email account. A few simple clicks should allow you easily add that sender to your address book and ensure they won't end up in spam or trash again.

If you notice that certain phrases keep hitting email messages with the spam filter and directing them away from your inbox, messages that you want to see, then you can go in and add a filter for that specific phrase or keyword. From there, you can choose for all messages with those properties (keyword, phrase, etc) never end up in the trash or spam folders in the future.

These are just a few simple ways you can be certain that you never miss important messages, regardless of their content and your spam filters.

---

## Creating An Address Book To Ensure Message Delivery

If you've been on the Internet for longer than a few hours (seriously!) then you've more than likely heard of the address book.

This is just a built-in feature with most e-mail service providers and clients that allows you to "white list" an e-mail address that contacts you.

When a contact is added to your address book, the white list allows their messages to ALWAYS get through to you. Additionally, you can also easily refer to their address or other details, and contact them more easily.

These address book details often sync to mobile phones as well for ease of use and simplicity (as is the case with Google Mail).

I won't go into detail about how to add contacts to your address book or fill out the details, as it differs for most e-mail service providers (in some way). You can easily just look in the help section for your e-mail account provider and find out how you can start using the address book feature to white-list e-mail addresses that contact you frequently.

Be mindful of the security factor that plays a role here in the address book though. A lot of services have protective measures put into place for the address book, but you should always take extra care when adding people to your address book. Just in case something negative DOES happen.

---

## Frugality With Sharing Your Email Address...

You may be wondering what the point of an e-mail address actually is if you aren't sharing it and using it as a communication tool. Well, you definitely are supposed to be using it that way, but it's important to be careful HOW you actually use it around the Internet.

For instance, when you sign up for a random website, forum, or mailing list; you never truly know who may be getting access to your email address at the end of the day.

While this may not seem like a big ordeal, it only takes one bad apple to sour the bunch. What that means is that maybe your email address falls into the wrong hands.

Here's a couple scenarios that could happen:

- The database of email addresses signed up for a website (forum, message board, etc) is compromised. Maybe the passwords were also revealed and 'stolen' by the hacker as well. Not only could they use software to rapidly check passwords (from the website's usernames, etc) towards email addresses, but they could also sell your email address to tons of spammers and that means an inbox full of junk.

- A list or website that you've signed up for has decided to release your email address to other individuals or companies. Whether it's for monetary compensation or the company is liquidated (or absorbed) - it happens every now and again. This basically spells out an entire array of spam for your nice clean inbox.

The above are just a few instances in which your email address could end up in a bad place, and even worse, you account details count end up compromised.

This doesn't necessarily mean that you should never use your email to sign up for different places or of course, to share with friends and family (etc). It just means you need to be far more conscious of where you are using your email.

One helpful suggestion is to create ANOTHER email account for signing up to different forums and services around the web. Then you can choose to FORWARD the emails from that account to your main email account.

Nearly all email providers will allow you to forward your emails from one address to another, along with a myriad of different forwarding options.

This means you can keep junk email exclusive to a different account and create extensive filters to take care of that. Allowing you to keep your main email account free and safe of that sort of compromise.

** NOTE: If you follow the steps in this course for setting up a secure password and account security question - you shouldn't have to worry as much about a user name and password database leak.

The topic of creating a secondary account and the main method for avoiding spam, hassles, and that kind of stuff has been talked about in depth.

Let's assume you don't always want to have to create a different email account for signing up to this and that. Maybe you don't want to fuss around with any of those tasks.

Let's say you just want a quick fix...

There are services that provide "throw away" email accounts or 10 minute accounts. These accounts serve an in-the-moment purpose of allowing you to use a disposable email that will expire after a short duration. Just long enough for you to sign up and confirm a subscription to get access to something.

Keep in mind though, this is somewhat frowned upon in

the marketing world, other niches and in many other situations. Sometimes autoresponder services will have built-in mechanisms to block registration using these kinds of email services. With that said, it's important to always remember that and be respectful.

Also make note that a lot of these services don't provide a password to your account, which is exactly why they should only be used for a quick fix and purpose and then tossed. Technically anybody can access them. Save any important information you may receive via email using these (log-ins, credentials, etc). Make sure to delete any information (emails with log-in details, etc) from the throwaway account afterward as well.

Anyway, in the event that you would like to use a throwaway email service, here is a list of just a few of the top providers:

- http://www.10minutemail.com - [ This is exactly

what it says, it lasts for 10 minutes and then expires. ]

- http://www.throwawaymail.com - [ Simple and free temporary email address generator. ]

- https://www.guerrillamail.com - [ Same as above, just a different name and a few different tools built in. ]

- http://www.mailinator.com - [ Been around for a long time and very well known. Sometimes these are marked as spam or filtered automatically. ]

- http://www.20minutemail.com - [ Similar to the first service but lasts for 20 minutes instead before expiring. ]

As mentioned before, make sure that you save any important information that you receive via inbox to these throwaway accounts. Then also delete the email from that inbox (as anybody could technically access your account if it's not expired).

You should really just make a second account (or use your main account) for things like signing up for:

- Forums
- Social Networks
- Important Websites
- Semi-Trusted Mailing Lists
- And so on...

Now that you're familiar with throwaway accounts, using a secondary account (with forwarding if necessary), and how to filter and manage your inbox - it's time to move forward toward additional preventative measures in securing not only your personal information but also your email accounts and any other account on the web.

---

## Protecting Personal Information...

9 time out of 10 when you're signing up for an email

account, social network, or a plethora of other websites on the world wide web - you'll be asked the inevitable: what is your birth date?

Advancing personal questions even more, sometimes you'll be asked things like your full name (obviously), your location or birth place (sometimes for security question), hobbies, and any other random questions.

While most of these are standard procedure and you shouldn't give it a second thought, maybe you actually SHOULD think about it carefully.

Where are you signing up to? If it's for your email account, keep in mind that you may need to know the information you're providing.

For instance, sometimes when resetting or recovering your password, you may need to enter your birthday (or the birth date you chose for your account). Because of this, you need to realize that if you sign up anywhere on the web or communicate your birthday anywhere on the web, publicly (or not), people might be able to see that information.

As mentioned previously throughout this course, details such as the following are not uncommon to be asked during the registration process. Or even in the case of social networks and personal connection sites. And they can quite often also be related to account security related questions, which translates to headaches and danger for you or your account (in some cases).

Commonly requested details (often used for account security in other places):
- What is your birthday?
- What is your mother's maiden name?
- What is your favorite color?
- What is your favorite food?
- In what city were you born?

- What street did you grow up on?
- What school did you attend for X grade?
- What was the make of your first car?
- And the list goes on (just see more here: https://www.quora.com/What-are-the-most-common-security-questions-to-retrieve-a-users-password )

While you may scoff at the idea that anybody would guess these or be able to decipher this information and use it to access your account, you'd be even more astounded at how often it really does occur.

By process of elimination, it's not out of line to see how a "hacker" could use the Internet to figure out what school you went to for 1st grade, or even what street you grew up on. Details as far as your mother's maiden name are not far out to uncover when using the Internet craftily to find bits of information.

These details can frequently be dug up somewhere on the web, somehow. Even further, they can often be guessed by just looking up common lists (as in the case of the make of a car). Maybe not in every individual person's case, but it's better to be safe rather than sorry.

Putting forth a little effort and preemptive thinking towards both current and future account creation and security management techniques can go a long way.

---

## Google+ (And Other Social Media) Security...

If you're using G-Mail (Google Mail) as your email service provider, then you will have a Google+ account automatically setup for you from the get go. This happens irregardless as to whether you wanted it to happen or not.

Guess what? Google+ shares a bunch of information about you that you may have filled in or set up over time.

If you're starting to panic now - don't worry just yet. You aren't fully in the danger zone yet.

What you should do is venture out to Google+ and then follow these steps after you're logged in with your main Gmail account.

1. Click on the "Home" button towards the upper left corner of the page. Select "Settings" from the list

that drops down.

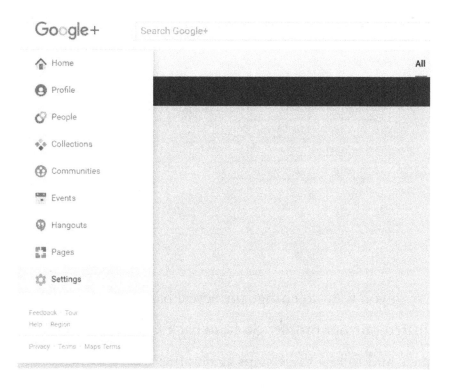

2. From the window that displays, scroll down to the "Profile" section.

3. Most of these options are self-explanatory but if you want to uncheck certain ones, you can follow this image:

**Profile**

*Show your Google+ communities posts on the Posts tab of your Google+ profile. Learn more.

Show these profile tabs to visitors (they're always visible to you): Learn more

- ✓ Photos
- ✓ YouTube / Videos
- ☐ +1
- ✓ Reviews

☐ Allow people to send you a message from your profile    Extended circles ⇕

☐ Help others discover my profile in search results. Learn more

Unchecking this box prevents most search engines from indexing your profile. It does not prevent them from indexing any public posts or comments.

☐ Show how many times your profile and content have been viewed.

Next, you want to change the actual basic information shared on your profile. So head back to Google+ home page and follow these steps again after you've logged in.

1. In the top left corner, click the drop-down menu that reads Home > and click Profile.

Go gle+     Search Google+

Home

Profile

People

Collections

Communities

Events

Hangouts

Pages

Settings

Feedback · Tour
Help · Region

Privacy · Terms · Maps Terms

All

2. Below your cover photo, click About > scroll to the box you want to edit.

3. In the lower left corner of the box, click Edit.

4. When you edit your information, use the drop-down menu on the right to decide who sees your information.

5. If you make changes, click Save in the bottom right corner.

Following these sets of steps should allow you to completely pick and choose what information is shared about you and exactly what information you even have out there floating around on the web via your Google+ profile. And believe it or not, Google+ definitely holds a lot of weight in the search results.

Keeping with the process of making your profile private - you can also venture out to websites like Facebook and such. Open the "Privacy" settings and make sure that the information you're sharing is the information that you're actually comfortable with sharing to the public (or even your friends on that network).

Make it a point to periodically check these settings both on your email (Gmail) account, and on many social media and networking websites as well. Sometimes these networks may update policies and push out other updates that mess with the privacy settings (especially on

Facebook).

Nowadays it's really common for websites to simplify the registration process for their actual site or community. Because of this, you will often be presented with the option to "sign up" or "log in" using various different popular social networks and accounts. This could include Facebook, Twitter, LinkedIn, Gmail, and so on.

This entire process is most often referred to as allowing third-party app access to your account.

This generally isn't much of an issue or concern. However, you need to be aware of the information that you're sharing with these networks when you initially sign up or log in to the site. You can almost always choose the exact information you're sharing with these sites (by selecting or deselecting little bubbles).

In the end, you will usually have to share something like

your e-mail, but that's not really much of an issue. If it is, you can always just sign up with a throwaway e-mail or a separate e-mail account all together.

Something that you SHOULD be aware of is the "third-party app" that is accessing your information. Use the same precautions for this type of thing as you would with sharing your personal e-mail. Don't use this method or share details with a suspicious looking site or a suspicious looking third-party app. Especially if it seems to be asking for A LOT of information during the sign up / integration process.

As a whole, you don't really have to be too concerned about allowing these third-party apps to have access or connect to your e-mail account or other social media account. It's usually just to extract the e-mail and allow you to bypass the registration process of filling out the forms.

Just be sure to emphasize caution with the sign up /
connection process, just as you would with sharing any
personal information or your e-mail account in any other
situation.

There is a chance you've actually encountered a similar situation to which the following information pertains.

Some email service providers, social media websites, and various other networks will often "force" you to change your password or other details related to your account every few months. Sometimes this may even happen as a result of a security breach or just a security update within the network.

This may seem like a hassle, and you run the possibility of forgetting your newly chosen password if you do change it. However, this is an excellent method to ensure that you account(s) always stay secure.

This is important because you see, not all "hackers" and security breaches take action on the accounts that they gain access to immediately.

In the event that a security breach may have leaked your password (amongst hundreds or even thousands of others), the receiver of said password may try and access your account months or even years down the road. If you've already changed your password - then they're fresh out of luck and locked out in the cold.

Some people come up with an algorithm for creating a unique password that you can always remember that somehow relates to the date or something similar. By doing a Google search for "Password creation methods" or "password creation algorithms" you can find plenty of information on the topic.

When it really comes down to it, you just need to keep up to date with the security aspects of not just your email account(s) but also any other important accounts that if compromised, could lead to a headache and lots of panic.

It's been previously mentioned about turning on mobile notifications and multi-step authentication for your account(s), and this is an excellent way to get live updates about potential security threats towards your account(s). If you haven't done so already, make sure that you at least look into the feature to see if your service provider supports it.

Making it a habit to stay up to date and get into a routine of checking privacy settings, log-in history, and other security factors will allow the overall process to become almost second nature to you. This means always having a secure network of accounts whether related to email, business, or anything else.

After going through the majority of this course, it's almost a given that you've been considering the security on other fronts. By other fronts, I'm referring to accounts related to payments (PayPal, Banks, Credit Cards), social media accounts, business accounts, and really any other account that may be connected to valuable information.

There's some good news and some bad news here though.

The goods news is that everything you've learned and can apply in this course can easily be put into action for any other account found on the web. All of this security mumbo-jumbo isn't just exclusive to e-mail accounts. As a matter of fact, you're more likely to run into far more (and higher) levels of security when dealing with payment based accounts such as banks and so on.

You can apply the password techniques, account security methods, and all of the additional security levels such as mobile phone, 2 step authentication and even on-the-go (mobile) alerts to any website out there that supports any of these features.

Now, the bad news is that SOME websites out there might not have as much or as many factors of security or even as much emphasis on security as they should. To combat this, you can utilize every feature that IS available to you. While also always being certain that you have an extremely strong password and even stronger account security question (and answer).

Another thing that almost all places (websites) out there support is the backup email address. You should take the time to visit many of the websites and networks that you frequently use and check to see if they have an emergency / recovery email address feature. Or even if they have a feature to retrieve your account via (mobile) phone number.

If it's an important account to you that contains or links to pertinent valuable information, then make it a habit of routinely checking up on the account's health and status. This can be as simple as logging in, checking past log-in activity (if supported), and even changing your password regularly.

Keeping a close watch over accounts and above all, ensuring that your security measures are the best they can be, will allow you to not only significantly prevent the chance of a security threat, but also allow you to be prepared in the event that something does happen.

## Dealing With A Disaster (Your Account Has Been Compromised - But Don't Panic!)...

So the unthinkable has happened: your (email) account has been compromised.

You're probably already in panic mode when you first realize it's happened. But that can just make the situation far worse than it has to be.

Yes, your personal information may be in jeopardy but that doesn't mean you can't remedy the situation with a clear mind and a quick actionable plan.

Let's say that you've taken all of the precautions explained in this course, and you receive a notification on your phone (you did set up mobile notifications, right?) that some foreign address has logged into your G-Mail account? (Side note: you ARE using Google Mail at this point, aren't you?)

- The first thing you need to do is remain calm. Get to a computer or a secure Internet connection as soon as possible.

- If you have access to any sort of financial or important accounts on your phone, check them to make sure they haven't also been compromised.

- Next, you want to be certain that the email account has actually been broken into. If it hasn't been, then you just need to make sure you update a few credentials when you can get to a computer (this will be covered later in this section).

Be careful not to immediately start to request password resets and start trying to move accounts off of your email account that was compromised. The reason for this is because if the "hacker" is monitoring the activity, they may take further steps to secure the account from YOU getting it back in your possession. They may also become aware of important accounts that were linked to your account because of the notifications you sent.

If you can't get to a computer in time, you are going to need to contact certain accounts by phone that you feel might be at risk. This can involve banks, PayPal, credit cards, and other monthly payment services too. Explain the situation to them and that you need to change your password and credentials, as well as your log-in email - because your email account that is linked to the account is compromised. They will almost always help you out with securing the account you're calling about (not the e-mail account, just the account you're calling about).

When you are finally on a secure computer and Internet connection again, you need to begin the process of trying to recover your account (if it has been broken into).

** Even if it hasn't been accessed, you should still take the time to go through and change your password, your security question, and any other details that you believe may have been revealed or at risk.

If your account has been accessed, you will want to start out by trying to request the password to the emergency / backup email that you created. That's why having the emergency account is so important. Furthermore, if you took the time to make sure the log-in details / credentials differ for the second account from your main account - the chances of the backup account being compromised are greatly decreased.

In order to request the password reset to your emergency account, you might have to answer a few personal questions about your account. If the intruder hasn't already figured out a way to change this information, you still have a high chance of recovering your account successfully. This is where you may be asked to enter details such as an account security question, birth date, maiden name, estimated date for when you created your email account, mobile phone number, backup email account address, and more. You may even be asked to confirm the reset via mobile phone.

If your security question has been changed, along with other details, they may not have gotten to the secondary email address and changed it yet. They may also have not changed the mobile phone connected to the account. So those 2 things are your next goal. Sometimes, if you can't get the questions correct, you can skip over them and are asked to input specific details like the mobile number or the exact recovery account address.

What you need to do is follow all of the steps that the account provider gives you towards getting your account back in your hands again. These may differ from website to website, but generally, the information that's been provided and covered in this course is what most of these websites and account providers use for account security and recovery.

Again, be sure to remain calm throughout the process, as becoming agitated or flustered can dilute the focus on your goal of securing your account.

As you can see, and have probably guessed - there are a number of ways to recover your account, and if you've taken the suggested precautions outlined in this course then you should already have everything at your fingertips necessary to get your account back in your possession.

If you've been successful in getting your account back, then you should immediately take the steps to go through and change all of the personal details. This includes passwords, account security question, birthday (if necessary), backup email (register a new one), and so on.

Check your "Outbox" or "Sent Messages" folder to see if the intruder sent or received any information or data before you were able to retrieve your account again.

You should also take the time to check on all of the accounts connected to this email account and make certain that they haven't also been accessed and compromised as well.

- If you've been unsuccessful in getting your account back, then you have a lot of work cut out for you. But remember, staying calm will allow this process to go by a lot easier than it would if you're upset.

First, you will want to register a new email account immediately, as well as a new backup account.

Start trying to log-in and gain access to any accounts that may be connected to your main (stolen) email account. Be very cautious in the methods you take as to not alert the hacker as to your activity and lower your chances of recovering attached accounts.

Update the connected emails to any accounts that were

connected to your stolen account and were not compromised as well. This means connecting them to your NEW email account.

If you have any financial accounts linked to your stolen email account and they have not been compromised - you need to make haste in logging in and changing the security details and credentials for each account. Move them to a new email address (the new one you created) and even request new credit cards and bank cards with new numbers to be extra safe.

In the event that any of your other accounts were compromised, you simply need to follow the same steps for trying to re-acquire those accounts as you have for your main e-mail account. As mentioned before, the steps and process may vary but for the most part, the information required to reset or re-gain access is usually the same across the board (web).

Once you've managed to move all of your uncompromised accounts to your new email account, changed passwords and security details, and such - you should make it a point to regularly monitor your new e-mail account and other accounts. At least for a few weeks or even months to make sure that nothing suspicious happens.

You should already be monitoring your accounts as it is, so this shouldn't be an issue. :)

Lastly, you want to contact any individuals or companies (to an extent) that may have had your stolen e-mail address in their address book and inform them of what happened. Tell them they should check the security of their account(s) and even change or update the log-in credentials just to be safe. Also let them know to inform you if they happen to receive any messages from your stolen e-mail account or even see any activity from the account.

Regardless of if you've followed all of the steps and information laid out in this course - there is ALWAYS going to be a level of risk involved with having an account on the Internet. Just like in life, there's always some sort of risk of some mishap occurring with just about everything.

The best thing you can do is take preemptive measures to secure your personal and important data and accounts, and be prepared in the case of something happening.

Best of luck to you in the future, and I hope your days (and years) are filled with entirely headache-free and non-threatening e-mail and account security encounters and usage.

## Resources List...

**Free Email Service Providers:**

Google's E-mail Service...
http://gmail.com

Outlook (Has Been Around For Ages)...
http://www.outlook.com

Yahoo's E-mail Service...
https://mail.yahoo.com/

Very Powerful And Popular Free E-mail Service...
http://www.inbox.com

Apple's Free Cloud Based E-mail Service...
https://www.icloud.com/mail

With a name like Mail.com – you know they're awesome...
http://www.mail.com

America Online's E-mail Service (Been Around Since The Beginning)...
https://my.screenname.aol.com

## Online Random Password Generators:

Quick and easy, simply click a button and you get an incredibly random and safe to use password...
https://lastpass.com/generatepassword.php

Complex and very customizable. Use this if you want to step up every bit of your password and even pass-phrase security with minimal effort...
http://passwordsgenerator.net/

Enter some information and click a button, for a randomized password...
https://www.random.org/passwords/

## Free Throwaway Email Service Providers:

This is exactly what it says, it lasts for 10 minutes and then expires...
http://www.10minutemail.com

Simple and free temporary email address generator...
http://www.throwawaymail.com

Same as above, just a different name and a few different tools built in...
https://www.guerrillamail.com

Been around for a long time and very well known. Sometimes these email addresses are marked as spam or filtered automatically...
http://www.mailinator.com

Similar to the first service but lasts for 20 minutes instead before expiring..
http://www.20minutemail.com

## Free Link Scanners:

This is an excellent and fast resource to quickly scan links.

http://scanurl.net/

Another free link / website scanner, but this time it's from Norton...
https://safeweb.norton.com/


## Other Reading:

Most common security questions...
https://www.quora.com/What-are-the-most-common-security-questions-to-retrieve-a-users-password

What to do if your account is compromised...
http://abcnews.go.com/Business/top-things-email-hacked/story?id=19715483#all

Dealing with a stolen account (it's for sure gone)...
http://us.norton.com/yoursecurityresource/detail.jsp?aid=email_hacked

## Password Creation References:

Four methods to create a secure password you'll actually remember...
http://lifehacker.com/four-methods-to-create-a-secure-password-youll-actually-1601854240

How to create a strong password (and remember it

too)...
http://www.howtogeek.com/195430/how-to-create-a-strong-password-and-remember-it/

7 Ways To Make Up Passwords That Are Memorable...
http://www.makeuseof.com/tag/7-ways-to-make-up-passwords-that-are-both-secure-memorable/

Don't make these common mistakes with your passwords...
http://www.komando.com/tips/9092/dont-make-these-common-mistakes-with-your-passwords/all


## Social Network Privacy Resources:

Privacy Rights Clearinghouse feature on Social Networking Privacy...
https://www.privacyrights.org/social-networking-privacy-how-be-safe-secure-and-social

Columbia Tech Report Regarding The Failure of Online Social Network Privacy Settings...
https://mice.cs.columbia.edu/getTechreport.php?techreportID=1459

Wiki regarding privacy concerns with social networking services...
https://en.wikipedia.org/wiki/Privacy_concerns_with_

social_networking_services

**Free Virus Scanners:**

http://free.avg.com/us-en/homepage

http://www.kaspersky.com/free-virus-scan

https://www.avast.com/en-us/index

# Account Security Basics Cheatsheet

The following checklist can apply to not just e-mail accounts but any account that you may want to improve the security.

## ☐ Account Details

☐ Birthday is either inaccurate or unknown to ANYBODY who may want access

☐ Multi-step authentication is enabled (Read more details here)

☐ Account / address is not shared publicly on any other websites

☐ If the account has a profile, make sure the profile is not public to ANYBODY

☐ If address contains name, ensure that the name cannot be used to gain access

## ☐ Password (Learn more here)

☐ Completely unique to your account and you

☐ Contains at least 1 capital letter

☐ Contains at least 1 symbol

☐ Contains at least 1 number / numeric

☐ Total length is at least 8 characters

# ☐ Account Security Question (See more details here)

☐ Question is unique to you and your account

☐ Answer is unable to be guessed, Googled, etc. by anybody

☐ Account / address is not shared publicly on any other websites

☐ If applicable, custom question was selected (Learn more: here)

☐ If applicable, answer is unique to question (See more details: here)

# ☐ Recovery Account Connected

☐ Does not have the same password as the main account

☐ Account security question is unique / different from main account

☐ Account / address is not shared publicly on any other websites

☐ Has no name based relevance or anything to the main account.

# ☐ Mobile Phone Number Connected

☐ Number has been verified and confirmed

☐ You have regular or constant access to the mobile phone

☐ Connected number is not publicly available on any websites or social media

☐ Mobile alerts have been enabled (for logging in from new locations and modifying account details)

☐ If applicable, 2-step authentication is enabled for your mobile number

# ☐ Account Details

☐ Privacy of e-mail account profile page is set to private (if applicable, learn more)

☐ Birthday, hometown, and current residence are not public anywhere

☐ Important account credentials (for your account or others linked) is saved locally or printed on paper

☐ Mobile notifications are enabled

# ☐ Preventative Measures

☐ Method created to remember password and security question answer and have them safely stored somewhere

☐ Logged into account regularly or have your email connected to your smart phone and set to auto-update

☐ If available, checked the login history (IP, location, etc.) for account(s)

☐ Backed up any important information or details found in your email inbox

☐ Personal information that could threaten your online security is set to private

## ☐ Additional Security

☐ Social networks are all private or do not share personal details or information

☐ Passwords are all unique for each account (universal password is NOT used)

☐ Emergency email or 2-step authentication is enabled on your account(s)

☐ Back-up email is also created for your main account's backup / recovery e-mail

# ☐ Disaster Checklist

☐ Remain calm

☐ Check if account has been fully compromised (yet)

☐ Determine if any other accounts have been compromised (yet)

☐ If accounts are compromised, contact financial accounts that may be linked to warn them of suspicious activity

☐ Get to a secure computer and Internet connection

☐ Check if your backup / emergency account is still safe

☐ Attempt to reset the password for compromised e-mail account

☐ Enter any requested information, if correct / successful, you should either be able to reset or receive reset request email to your backup address

☐ If successful in resetting the password, gain access to the account and change new password

☐ Check if other accounts are still compromised or not, and repeat the above steps to try and reset the password and restore your access

☐ Create new secondary e-mail account as a backup to your backup account and use the new account as the backup to your now re-acquired account

☐ Remain calm and continue to check regularly for any suspicious activity

☐ Emergency email or 2-step authentication is enabled on your account(s)

| Do's | Do Not's |
|---|---|
| Use a fully secure password (capital letters, symbols, numbers) | 4. Use the same password for multiple accounts (universal password) |
| Use a unique account security question answer | 5. Use the same account security question answer for multiple accounts |
| Connect a mobile number to your account | 6. Share your e-mail address publicly |
| Have a backup / secondary / recovery email account | 7. Sign up for suspicious opt-ins or mailing lists |
| Enable mobile notifications (for security) | 8. Click links in suspicious email messages |
| Use frugality when entering or signing up for websites or services with your email | 9. Reply to spam or suspicious messages |
| Implement usage of a "throwaway" email account service | 10. Share your password with anybody |
| Make use of a random password generator service (Learn more here) | 11. Reveal your personal information to anybody on the Internet |
| Come up with a method to remember your password or security question answer | 12. Publicly share your birthday, birth place, or current address |
| Store or print out | 13. Write your password anywhere on paper (in real life) where it |

| Do's | Do Not's |
|---|---|
| important emails or information received via e-mail | could be found by anybody else |
| Create both filters and folders for spam or even important messages (that you want to keep) | 14. Use your password as your account security question's answer |
| Regularly check any e-mail accounts that you own (as well as other accounts) to ensure their safety | 15. Store important information that can't be replaced or re-accessed in your inbox |
| Routinely change your passwords and account security question answer every 6-12 months (don't forget the new credentials though!) | 16. Forget to log out of your e-mail account when done on any computer |
| | 17. Allow any suspicious or untrusted apps to gain access to your account |
| Find a safe place to write down or store your password and account security question answer (along with other account or recovery based information) | 18. Panic if a disaster or security threat occurs |
| | 19. *OPTIONAL* Leave your information (password) stored on any computer (even your own) |

# Account Security Basics Quick Facts

In 2015, Symantec blocked 100 million FAKE technical support scams overall.

The US Government has $14 billion budgeted for cybersecurity in 2016.

The cyber insurance market has grown from $1 billion to $2.5 billion over the past two years

The cybersecurity workforce shortage is expected to reach 1.5 million unfilled positions by 2019.

Over $1 billion is being spent annually on security awareness training.

The global managed security services market is expected to grow from $8 billion in 2015 to $30 billion by 2020

Estimates show that IT security spending will soar from $75 billion-plus in 2015 to $101 billion in 2018.

Cyber-crime costs are projected to quadruple over the next few years and reach $2 trillion by 2019

More than half of the funds stolen through cyber-crime will NEVER be recovered.

As much as 70 percent of cyberattacks use a combination of phishing and hacking techniques.

In 2015, there were 38 percent more security incidents detected than in 2014.

Only 38 percent of global organizations claim they are prepared to handle a sophisticated cyberattack.

Over 169 million personal records were exposed in 2015, stemming from 781 publicized breaches.

The median number of days that attackers stay dormant within a network before detection is over 200

In April 2016, it was reported that the 71.1% of motivation behind attacks were cyber-crime based.

# About the Author: Bill Price

Bill Price is a Language Coach, blogger, polyglot, and lifelong language learner. He is the founder and creator of How To Languages, a language learning blog and publishing company. He is proficient in English, German, French, and Mandarin Chinese. He has also studied Cantonese, Farsi, Russian, Spanish, and Swahili to varying degrees. He currently resides in Denver, CO USA with his wife, Kirsten, and three children.

**Website/Blog:** www.BillPriceBooks.com
**Facebook:** www.facebook.com/BillPriceBooks
**Twitter:** www.twitter.com/AuthorBillPrice

**To inquire about personal language coaching, please email:** Bill@ideaseedlabs.com